The Good to Greek

Copyright

Copyright © Isabella Crasto 2013
Published by Isabella Crasto
All rights reserved
Second Edition 2013
ISBN: 978-1-291-44423-0

Contents

Statutory Warning

A Brief Introduction

First the Boring Bits

Pronunciation Guide Part 1 – The Greek Alphabet

Pronunciation Guide Part 2 – Accent Marks

At Last! Greetings and the Important Bits

Dining & Drinking Related

Potentially Hazardous Expressons

Some Related Words, Just For Good Fun

Quiz Time Answers

And in Conclusion

Appendix 1 – A Simple Guide to Pronunciation of the English Alphabet

Statutory warning

No prior knowledge of the Greek language required. Batteries not included. Do not use while bathing. Not suitable as a personal flotation device. Void where prohibited. Slippery when wet. Shake well before use. One size fits all. No salt, MSG, or artificial colour added. Contents may have settled during shipment. Not dishwasher safe. Do not use while sleeping. Contains no fruit juice. May contain traces of peanuts and wine. If swallowed, seek medical advice immediately. These premises are monitored by CCTV. No user–serviceable parts inside. Overdose may cause drowsiness. Follow directions inside. Sanitized for your protection. Do not use while operating a motor vehicle or heavy equipment. Parental discretion advised. Contains words related to sex. May not be suitable for persons under the age of three. Do not remove this tag under penalty of law. Do not use intimately. No other warranty, express or implied.

A Brief Introduction

When we came to Greece, we took some language courses and of course bought several introductory language books. They were good, but they were all missing something. We noticed this while dining out, relaxing in our village kafenion having cool frappés, and even while shopping. Little of what we were hearing so frequently quite matched what we had learned from our books, namely the myriad of daily greetings and polite expressions of warmth and kindness. So we began compiling a list of these, asking our friends (and sometimes complete strangers) for clarification or explanation. And we found ourselves using these expressions in everyday situations. It turned out to be a very useful exercise! We were no longer complete foreigners here. And we continue to be disappointed to see (or rather hear) people who have lived in Greece for more time than we have not even being able to say please or thank you correctly.

This book is the product of several years of careful observation, and many errors along the way! We would like to thank Eleni and Maria for their invaluable help in editing our efforts.

As opposed to the tone of most language learning texts, we have tried to make it fun and easy to follow. We hope you will enjoy reading this Good Guide to Greek and that you will find it useful during your stay in our adopted country, Greece.

First the Boring Bits

The Good Guide to Greek (or Γ³ in Greek) was prepared to aid the visitor to Greece (and new residents here as well) in the appropriate use of some basic greetings and pleasantries, most based on a single adjective: Kalos / Kalee / Kalo (in Greek, Καλώς / Καλή / Καλό). All three of these means good or fine. In fact, that's why the title of the book is the *Good* Guide to Greek. The *Bad* Guide to Greek would of course focus on the Greek word for bad, Κακός / Κακή / Κακό (Kakos / Kakee / Kako). But this wouldn't be so useful would it?

After your first few days in Greece, you will find that the Greeks greet each other with regularity ... there are literally hundreds of basic greetings and wishes; they are all used with great frequency. We theorize that one of the reasons why things move so slowly in Greece is that by the time the daily litany of greetings are over, there is little time or energy left to do anything else! But then that's a separate issue we don't have time to explore.

In English, the words "good" and "fine" are of course adjectives. That's our first word on grammar, and this little section will complete what must be said about this incessantly boring topic. Now, we all know that adjectives modify nouns, don't we? Nouns in English have no gender ... a chair is a chair and wine is wine. A fine chair is just a fine chair. And a good wine is of course a good wine. Alas that too is another subject and we shall make time for it very soon!

Greek nouns on the other hand are one of three genders: masculine, feminine, or neuter. The word for chair happens to be feminine while that for wine is neuter. And of course the adjective modifying a noun must agree with that noun. This is necessary we understand so there won't be a plethora of disagreeable nouns. That sounds rather nasty so we too must agree.

In Greek, it is not difficult at all to tell the ~~sex~~ gender of the noun. The article used before the noun gives it away completely so there are no surprises, well not yet at least. For example:

- Ο Άνδρας (O Andras) means "the man." The Greek article O in front not only means "the" but it also means that the "the" is a he "the," in other words, masculine.

- Η Γυναίκα (Ee Geeneka) means "the woman." The Greek article H (pronounced like the double "e" in bee or fee) means "the" again, but this time it's a she "the," or grammatically speaking, feminine. See the difference?

- Το Παιδί (To Pethi) means "the child." The Greek article "To" (pronounced like toe) means "the" yet again but this time it's a neuter "the." Perhaps the child is wearing a yellow jumper you say? Well, it doesn't matter. Some nouns in Greek, such as the words for child, wine, and tyre (or "tire" if you're from the colonies) are neuter. It's all Greek to me you say. Correct! 10 out of 10.

We hope this is clear so far. It can only get worse. If you are totally fed up already, take this little tome back and try to return it for a refund. Using some of the pleasantries given later will of course improve your chances of a refund, but then that wouldn't be cricket, would it?

Actually it gets seriously worse as a lot of the time the article "the" is dropped or used in a different form so we have to find another way 'round this. A good friend of ours has found a hidden connection between *what the thing is* and its gender. All a matter of careful observation she says. For example, the words for father, son, grandfather, uncle, and third nephew on my mother's side are all masculine. Similarly the words for mother, daughter, grandmother, aunt, and third niece on my mother's side are all feminine. How clever. But wait ... it gets better! By a simple extension of this basic observational technique (she insists) one could correctly ascertain that the words for tobacco, fever, wind, bakery, and danger are all masculine and that the words for sugar, night, blanket, kitchen, door, and victory are all feminine. Somehow we fail to grasp this simple extension and eagerly await her forthcoming book "Everything You Always Wanted to Know About Sex in Greek Grammar." Ένα καλό βιβλίο. A good book. Sounds like a winner!

Enough! All that was merely to explain why we have the *single* adjective Kalos / Kalee / Kalo (Καλώς / Καλή / Καλό) and they ALL mean good. There are good masculine things, good feminine things, and of course good neuter things.

If the reader has no interest at all in grammar (or sex), he/she/it is advised to skip the preceding section. We did warn you at the beginning it was boring!

Enough of this nonsense (literally) ... let's get to the meat (το κρέας – you just knew it was neuter didn't you) of the matter at hand!

Pronunciation Guide Part 1 – The Greek Alphabet

The English alphabet has 26 letters while the Greek alphabet has but 24, so it's in theory about 8% easier. And there are five vowels / vowel combinations that are pronounced as a long "e", as in "seed." And two vowels that are pronounced as a long "o" as in "boat". Ooops! Well, "oa" sounds like a long "o"! English ain't so simple either!

So, here's the Greek alphabet (with the names of the Greek letters) from alpha to omega with some guides to pronunciation when reading Greek words. Greek is very much WYSIWYG ... what you see is what you get, or more correctly what you read is exactly how you pronounce it. Unfortunately English lacks this very useful feature.

We have heard it said that the Greek system of writing is not only the most precise and perfect, but also the easiest in all the world, since it can be learned in 30 minutes. I think it was a Greek who said that however. Not doubt somewhat biased. But seriously, it is a whole lot easier to learn to read than English. Really! Try it and see.

There are some very comprehensive websites with nifty audio files so you can make well–informed mispronunciations!

1. Α – α (alpha)   as in when you say **ah** at the doctor's office. Please don't pronounce this letter sound as the Americans do (the short "a" in cat or hat)!

2. Β – β (veeta)   as in **v**itamin. No, it is not like the English "B/b" as in ball. The sound of the English B is made in Greek by a combination on consonants, Μ/μ and Π/π. More on this later.

3. Γ – γ (ghamma)   this letter has no equivalent in English. It is a bit like a soft **gh**a as a baby might gurgle; not a hard **g**oo but a soft **gh**a, To make matters worse, when it occurs before the letters E–ε, H–η, I–ι, or Y–υ it is pronounced sort of like the "y" in **y**ell. It is not pronounced as the English G in goat.

4. Δ – δ (thelta)   th, as in **the.** It is definitely not D as in definitely! However there is a consonant combination (ντ) that IS pronounced like D in English. So, ***QUIZ TIME***! After you have reached the last letter of the alphabet, try to remember to come back and read these two words out loud: Ντοναλντ Ντακ. What do they say? Answer at the end of this book. No peeking!!

5. E – ε (epseelon)   short e, as in b**e**d, s**ai**d, h**ea**d This English WYSIWY **don't** G! There is another short e in Greek, the vowel combination αι. It is pronounced exactly the same.

6. Z – ζ (zeeta)   as in **z**ebra. Why is Z here near the starting line and not at the end of the alphabet? Learn this and many more interesting facts about the Greek language in the book "Learn Greek in 25 Years." An excellent read! More so if you are 25 years younger than your current life expectancy.

7. H – η (eeta)   the first of the long e sounds, as in s**ee**d

8. θ – θ (theeta)   th (again), but this time as in the word **th**ree, not **th**e. Notice the difference when you say The Three Pigs. Go back four spaces to the Greek letter Δ–δ to see the difference.

9. Ι – ι (eeota)   another long e, as in s**ee**d

10. Κ – κ (kappa)   as in **k**it

11. Λ – λ (lamtha) as in **l**it

12. Μ – μ (mee)   as in **m**um. Remember the sound of the English letter B is a combination of this consonant plus Π/ π.

13. Ν – ν (nee)   as in **n**umb. You do remember that the consonant combination ΝΤ/ντ is pronounced like "D" English, don't you?

14. Ξ – ξ (ksee)   sounds like 'ks', as in fo**x**

15. Ο – ο (omeekron)   long o, as in b**oa**t

16. Π – π (pee)   as in **p**apa. For the mathematically inclined, please note that the name of the letter (in Greek) is pronounced "pee", not "pie" as made with apples or mince. Also you do remember that the consonant combination ΜΠ/μπ is pronounced like "B" English, don't you? Good. *QUIZ TIME* again! What fruit is represented by the Greek word μπανανα? [Hint: I don't think pies are made from this fruit.] Tick, tock, tick, tock, tick, tock ... Answer toward the end of this book.

17. P – ρ (rho)   as in **r**ed

18. Σ – σ – ς (sigma)   as is **s**eed. The lowercase ς is used only at the end of a word. The σ is used in all other positions.

19. T – τ (taf)   as in **t**an

20. Y – υ (eepseelon)   yet another long e, as in s**ee**d. It is perhaps interesting to note, well, maybe not so interesting, but anyhow, I digress. We've only got one vowel left and as a sneak preview, it's another "o." We've seen the English equivalents of only a, e, and o. So it may seem that Greek is a few beers short of a six–pack or a span short of a bridge? What about the vowel sound "u", as in y**ou**?? The vowel combination OY / ου is this missing link. And the long "i" sound as in "I am bored stiff right now?" Have patience … it's coming.

21. Φ – φ (fee)   as in **f**og

22. X – χ (hee)   pronounced something like the ch in Ba**ch**. We live near the city of Χανιά. In English, it is most often written as Chania. The "ch" is not pronounced as in **ch**ew but rather as in Ba**ch**.

23. Ψ – ψ (psee)   sounds like ps as in soa**ps**

24. Ω – ω (omayga)   bringing up the rear, yet another long "o" as in b**oa**t.

There are two more vowel combinations(ει and οι) that are also pronounced as a long "e." So there are five of theeeeese eeeees (Η/η, Ι/ι, Υ/υ, ΕΙ/ει, and ΟΙ/οι). In actual fact, Greeks are notoriously bad spellers. Who can blame them? Oh for Esperanto!

A small side note here ... just to further muddy the waters. As noted above, the vowel combination ΑΙ/αι is pronounced exactly like the fifth letter of the Greek alphabet, Ε/ε. But if there are two dots above the second vowel (like this: αϊ), each vowel is pronounced separately. For the passionate grammarian, I think this is called a diaeresis. But then maybe that is what you get from eating bad shellfish?

A bit more on the subject of αϊ. Say each letter separately and slowly ... ah–ee. Try it again, faster. Bet you have guessed by now it's *QUIZ TIME* yet again! The Greek αϊ is pronounced like which English vowel?

There are two more vowel combinations that you will come across frequently, αυ and ευ. These are pronounced as (1) af and ef, or (2) av and ev. The rules governing the choice are far too complex for this simple tome. For now, we'll leave it to chance!

And there are other consonant combinations to give us some missing sounds, such as the hard English G as in game. That's ΓΚ/γκ. The sound of the English letter J is also missing. In Greek it is approximated by ΤΖ/τζ. There are a few more but we can safely overlook these for now. Just pronounce the two consonants together quickly and it'll be close enough. One can stumble and mumble along okay without this unnecessary confusion.

[In case you forgot, now would probably be a good time to go back to the Greek letter Δ/δ and take the quiz. No pressure mind you; there are no CCTV cameras installed despite an earlier warning.

Okay, clear as mud you say. Good, so let's move on. But before we do, it's *QUIZ TIME* yet again! You may see this word printed on signboards, particularly hair dressing salons, and restaurants. Kan u pronownse it korrectly?

    PANTEBOY

Answer at the end of this book. No peeking!!

Pronunciation Guide Part 2 – Accent Marks

Well, we are almost ~~threw~~ through with learning how to read and pronounce Greek words. Has this taken more than 30 minutes? Less than 25 years we hope!

Modern Greek is written with accent marks to help pronounce the word correctly. In English, there are a number of instances where two different words share the same spelling but have two different meanings and may have different pronunciations.

Read and read for example. There are many of these in English. Minute (1/60th of an hour) and minute (small), wave (hello there!) and wave (what surfers love), and so on. These are called homographs. Really … I looked it up!

The folks who invented modern Greek were far–sighted enough to avoid this problem by applying accent marks. Thus we have yeros and yeros (in Greek, γέρος and γερός). The former, pronounced with the accent on the first syllable (ye'ros) means "strong." The latter, pronounced with the accent on the last syllable (ye–ros'), means "old man". So of course it follows that Ο γέρος γερός means the strong old man. And we are certain that having diligently applied the rules from the previous section, you have made the correct choice that the guy is masculine! The whole point of this nonsense is that we will put accent marks after the stressed syllable to help you pronounce the words with reasonable precision. Or, perhaps less clearly, *ac'–cent the syl'–la–ble that has the a–pos'–trophe fol'–low–ing it.* There's no point in seeing a strong young buck and calling out to him "Wow – γερός!" You've just blown your chance!

At Last! Greetings and the Important Bits

The Greeks by nature are a very friendly people, except perhaps when driving. If you fail to notice this during your stay, well, you must be wearing very dark sunglasses and have cotton in your ears. We are of course biased and believe the Greeks to be among the most generous and kind–hearted people on earth. Stay a while and you may find that you agree. So, in an effort to return the kindnesses proffered, we believe that employing a few kind words in Greek will help to make your stay more enjoyable. Plus it will certainly warm the hearts of the Greek men and women and children whom you meet in passing. You can probably forget all the boring bits on grammar. Try to get the pronunciation close. And most of all have fun!

We wish you a most pleasant time in Greece. Καλώς ήρθατε και καλές διακοπές!

- Καλώς ήρθατε – Welcome! – *Ka–los' Eer'–tha–te!*

- Καλώς ορίσατε – Welcome! – *Ka–los' Or–ee–sa–te!*

You'll hear these expressions often. The most appropriate response is to say thank you. In Greek, that's

- Ευχαριστώ – *Ef–har–ee–sto'*

In the transliterations, a single "e" is pronounced like the "e" in "bet. The double "ee" is pronounced as in bee, fee, see. The "a" is short, as in ah or far.

- Παρακαλώ – (*pa–ra–ka–lo'*) A very useful word; it means please, as in "Please get on with it!"

- Λυπάμαι – (*lee–pa'–me*) means I'm sorry (for something that wasn't your fault)

- Συγγνώμη – (*seeg–no'–mee*) also means I'm sorry or excuse me (for something I did like stepping on your toe!)

Let's move on to daily greetings, more in less in chronological order:

- Καλημέρα – Good morning or good day – *Ka–lee–mer'–a*

- Καλησπέρα – Good evening – *Ka–lee–sper'–a*

- Καληνύχτα – Good night – *Ka–lee–neech'–ta*

Don't forget that the Greek letter X / χ is pronounced as the "ch" in Bach. So the third syllable in the word above is not pronounced as the English word "niche." Try to say the *nee* bit and then end it with Bach's *ch*.

You can use Καλημέρα up until 4 pm or so, but see more options below. After dark, use Καλησπέρα. On parting in the evening, use Καληνύχτα.

To get you through the rest of the day, here's a few more:

- Καλό μεσημέρι – Good midday – *Ka–lo' me–see–mer'–ee*

    Use this one between noon and about 4 pm.

- Καλό απόγευμα – Good afternoon – *Ka–lo' a–po'–gev–ma*

This is suitable between say 4 pm until before sunset.

In the transliterations, a single "o" is pronounced like oh.

A useful reply to these (and others as appropriate!) is

- Επίσης – And to you – *E–pee'–sees*

Keep a calendar handy ... the following are very useful on Mondays and on the first day of the month. You'll always get a warm Επίσης from these!

- Καλή εβδομάδα – Have a good week! – *Ka–lee' ev–tho–ma'–tha* (on Mondays)

Note again that the Greek letter δ (delta) is NOT pronounced as the English "D" but rather more like "th" as in the word "the."

- Καλό μήνα – Have a good month! – *Ka–lo' mee'–va* (on the first of the month)

And, if the first of the month happens to be a Monday, use both!

And from Friday afternoon until Saturday evening you can use the following:

- Καλό Σαββατοκύριακο – Have a good weekend! – *Ka–lo' Sav–va–to–kee'–ree–a–ko*

And of course if you happen to be here during any of the big holidays:

- Καλή Χρονιά – Happy New Year! – *Ka–lee' chron–yee–a'* Again, remember that the Greek Χ/χ is pronounced as the "ch" in Bach.

- Καλες Απόκριες – Happy Carnival! – *Ka–les' A–po'–kree–es*

- Καλή Σαρακοστή – Happy 40 days until Easter! – *Ka–lee' Sa–ra–kos–tee'*

- Καλό Πάσχα – Happy Easter! – *Ka–lo' Pas'–cha* This is used in the weeks leading up to Good Friday.

- Καλή Ανάσταση – Happy Ressurection! – *Ka–lee' A–na'–sta–see* Use this from Good Friday after the evening church service though Easter Sunday.

- Καλά Χριστούγεννα – Merry Christmas! – *Ka–la' Chree–stoo'–yen–na.* Remember that the vowel combination ου pronounced as the ou in y**ou**.

- Καλές γιορτές– wish you nice holidays! – *Ka–les' yee–or–tes'*

And more! Are you beginning to see why everything moves so slowly here??

- Καλό καλοκαίρι – Have a good summer! – *Ka–lo' ka–lo–ker'–ee*

- Καλό χειμώνα – Have a good winter! – *Ka–lo' chee–mo'–na*

- Καλά στέφανα – Happy Wedding!– *Ka–la' Ste'–fa–na*

- Καλούς απογόνους – Have good children! – *Ka–lous' a–po–go'–noos*

- Καλή επέτειος – Happy Anniversary! – *Ka–la' e–pe'–tee–os*

- Καλά γενέθλια – Happy Birthday! – *Ka–la' ge–ne'–thlee–a*

- Also Πολίχρονος – Live for many years! This is more appropriate for adult birthdays. *Po–lee'–chron–os*

There is another greeting that is used for birthdays and anniversaries:

- Να ζήσετε! – *Na zee'–se–te* meaning live happily. This is a very general and multi–purpose greeting. Use anytime to parents with small children, for birthdays, anniversaries, at weddings, etc.

To the friend or acquaintance who has just bought a new car, boat, airplane, etc:

- Καλορίζικο – Congratulations! Good luck! – *Ka–lo–ree'–see–ko*

To friends leaving the kafenion:

- Καλή αντάμωση – Until we meet again – *a–da'–mo–see*

- Καλή βόλτα – Have a good stroll! – *vol'–ta*

- Καλή δουλειά – Good working! (if headed directly back to work) – *thoo–lee–a'*

- Καλές διακοπές – Enjoy your holidays – *thee–a–ko–pes'*

- Καλό δρόμο – Have a good drive! – *thro'–mo*

- Καλό ταξίδι – Have a good trip! – *taks–ee'–thee*

- Καλό μπάνιο – Enjoy your swim! (assuming they are headed straight to the beach without a long walk and not going by motorbike) – *ban'–ee–o*

- Καλόν ύπνο – Sleep well! (assuming they are neither going swimming first nor driving a long way on a motorbike to reach the place where you're wishing them to sleep well … it can get complicated!) – *eep'–no*

- Στο καλό – Go well! If you haven't a clue what to say, this is perfect for all occasions! – *Sto ka–lo'*

And yet more:

- Καλό περπάτημα – Have a good walk! – *per–pat'–ee–ma*

- Καλό ξενύχτι – Have a good night out! – *ksen–ee'–chtee*

- Καλά να περάσατε – Have fun! Enjoy! Take it easy! – *na per–a'–sa–te*

- Καλή επιτυχία – Good luck! – *epee–tee–chee'–a*

- Καλή τύχη – Good luck! – *tee'–chee*

- Καλή διασκέδαση – Have a good time! – *thi–a–ske'–tha–see*

- Καλή πρόοδο – Good progress or good advances! (to a student in his or her studies) – *pro'–o–tho*

- Με το καλό – Have it in a good way! (for a new house, marriage, graduation, etc) – *Me to ka–lo'*

- Καλές διακοπές – Have a good holiday/vacation! – *thee–a–ko–pes'*

- Καλή διαμονή – Enjoy your stay! – *thee–a–mon–ee'*

- Καλή συνέχεια – May good continue! This is useful when leaving a shop after buying something, or when saying goodbye to a friend. – *see–ne'–chee–a*

- Καλή προπόνηση – Good workout/training! – *pro–po'–nee–see*

- Καλή πρωτομαγιά – Good first of May! – *pro–to–ma–yee–a'*

May 1st is a holiday here. We eat, drink, and enjoy the fine spring weather. The children make flower wreathes.

To a lady before her wedding:

- Η ώρα η καλή – The time is good – *Ee o'–ra ee ka–lee'*

- Με το καλό ο γάμο σας! – We wish you well for your wedding! – *Me to ka–lo' o ga'–mo sas*

To women who are pregnant or have recently given birth:

- Καλή ελευτεριά – literally wish you good freedom – *e–lev–te–ree–a'*

- Καλά γεννητούρια – literally wish you a painless birth – *yen–nee–too'–ree–a*

- Καλά σαράντα – literally Happy Forty – *sa–ran'–da*

The first is a wish for having a smooth pregnancy and release from the problems it may have caused. The last can be used any time during the 40 days following birth. The mother and child usually stay at home during this period.

Dining & drinking–related

- Καλό δείπνο – Have a good dinner! – *theep'–no*

- Καλή όρεξη – Good appetite! – *or'–e–ksee*

- Καλό κουράγιο! or just plain Κουράγιο! – Keep your courage! (appropriate after the fifth chikoudia) – *koo–ra'–gee–o*

- Also Καλή δύναμη – Keep your strength! – *thee'–na–mee*

- Καλή τύχη – Good luck! – *tee'–chee* (for anyone in need of luck, such as navigating to the correct hotel room from the taverna after a particularly long evening of elbow-bending)

- Καλό ξημέρωμα – Good dawn / Good rising! This has nothing to do with baking bread but is said on parting in the evening as wishes for the next morning. After a friend has had a few too many ouzos, this is an appropriate way to say farewell – *ksee–mer'–o–ma*

- Καλή ανάρρωση – Get well soon! – *a–na'–ro–see* (may be appropriate on the morning after). You can also say Περαστικά (*per–as–tee–ka'*) to someone who is ill, or hungover!

Potentially hazardous expressions

- Καλό κυνήγι – Good hunting! – *kee–nee'–gee.* Hunting in rural Greece, and most especially in Crete, is a favourite pastime. The most frequent targets seem to be road signs although we have heard that a few birds actually are targeted, and not a few fellow hunters. Use this expression with caution, especially if you're standing near a road sign!

- Καλό πλεκτό – Good knitting! – *plek–to'* Considerably safer than the one above. But not to a chap with a hunting rifle please, unless he's standing next to his grandmother who happens to be knitting *and* you're not standing in front of a road sign!

And finally, a true story. Each year the local Orthodox priest blesses the homes in our village. Last year the priest visited and performed the usual ceremonies and ended with a slightly modified version of his blessings to our neighbours (husband, wife, and two sons aged 8 and 17:

- To the parents: Καλή συνέχεια! – May good continue!

- To the 8–year old: Καλή πρόοδο! – Good advancement (in his studies)!

- And to the 17–year old: Καλές σούζες! – Good wheelies (with his motorcycle)!

Some related words, just for good fun!

- Καλά (*Ka–la'*) is an adverb meaning fine, good, or well.

- Καλά είμαι (*Ka–la' ee'–me*) means I am fine.

- Καλά είμαστε (*Ka–la' ee'–mas–te*) means we are fine.

- Καλοκαίρι (*Ka–lo–ke'–ree*) means summer and comes from our good word Καλο plus καίρος which means weather.

- Κάνει καλό καιρό means "It's good weather" *(Ka'–nee ka–lo' ke–ro')*

- Καλός / Καλύτερος / Ο καλύτερος – Yes, you guessed it. These three adjectives mean Good / Better / Best. Be careful to make the genders agree, but of course you already *know* that!

On a more sombre note, here are three expressions for bereavement:

- Συλληπτήρια – Our condolences – *See–leep–tee'–ree–a*

- Ζωή σε εσάς – May your life go on – *Zo–ee' se e–sas'*

- Να ζείτε να τον / την θυμάσαστε – Live to remember him (τον) or her (την) *Na zee–te na ton / teen thee–ma'–sa–te*

And two for those who are ill or troubled:

- Περαστικά! – Get well! (to someone or for someone who is sick or unwell) – *(per–as–tee–ka´)*

- Σιδερένιος! – Be strong! (use as above or to/for someone who is troubled) – *See–der–e´–nee–os*. The Greek word for iron is σίδερο *(see´–der–o)*

Quiz Time Answers

Question Number 1. Pronounce these two words: Ντοναλντ Ντακ. If you guessed Mickey Mouse, you're close but no cigar. Try again!

Question Number 2: What fruit is represented by the Greek word μπανανα? Correct!

Question Number 3: The Greek vowel combination αῐ sounds like which English vowel? Sorry to disappoint but we're not going to give you the answer directly. It's in one of the following WYSI not WYG English words: eight, bead, aisle, goat, through. So did you manage to find the last missing vowel sound in Greek that we were blabbering on about before? Μπάβο!

Question Number 4: How to pronounce the Greek word PANTEBOY (or ραντεβου written in lower case). You guessed it! **Rendezvous**. See how easy it is to read the Greek. Try explaining to someone why we pronounce the sequence of letters r–e–n–d–e–z–v–o–u–s as we do. And don't blame the French either!

And in conclusion

Now that you have all this under your belt, there is so much more to learn and have fun with. A next logical step would be to take up the word POLI (πολλοί / πολλές / πολλά) meaning many, and it's adverbial relative POLI (πολύ) meaning very. That's the subject of our next book Π3 which, based on reviews from this first effort, will probably never be written.

A wonderfully useful snippet from this book–probably–never–to–be is

- Χρόνια πολλά (Ch*ron'–ee–a pol–la'*) which is a greeting used on Christmas Day, New Year's Day, and on anyone's birthday and name day. It's very handy. Don't leave home without it!!

And a few more very useful expressions:

- Πολύ καλό!– Very good! – *Po–lee' ka–lo'* – Use this anywhere and everywhere, very commonly with Ευχαριστώ (thank you).

- Πολύ ωραίο – Very nice! – *Po–lee' o–re'–o*

- Πολύ νόστιμο! Delicious! Very tasty! – *Po–lee' no'–stee–mo*

Thanks for bearing with us! We hope at least some of the information here will be useful to you during your stay in Greece. Tell your friends if you like, however we disclaim all liability for the resultant loss of friendship. You can try to <u>click here</u> to rate this book.

☺ ☺ ☺ ☺ ☺   Magnificent – kept me and the mozzies in my bedroom up all night

☺ ☺ ☺ ☺   Stunning – kept me somewhat close to the edge of my seat

☺ ☺ ☺   Wonderful – also useful as a fly swatter

☺ ☺   Glorious – useful to save bookmarks and flatten 5 Euro notes

☺   Brilliant – when pre–soaked slightly, it's a substitute for toilet paper

For those of you who purchased the electronic version of this tome, we apologise for the inconvenience.

Appendix 1

A Simple Pronunciation Guide to the English Alphabet

We thought it would be appropriate to include here a section explaining how to pronounce the sounds of the letters in the English alphabet. You can compare this with the Greek alphabet, and perhaps see if we have made our point.

- **A** as in Aisle
- **B** as in Bdellium
- **C** as in Czar
- **D** as in Djakarta
- **E** as in Eight
- **F** as in Philadelphia
- **G** as in Gnat
- **H** as in Honor
- **I** as in Seize
- **J** as in Juarez
- **K** as in Knight
- **L** as in Would
- **M** as in Mnemonic
- **N** as in Solemn
- **O** as in Phoenix

- **P** as in Pneumonia
- **Q** as in Quay
- **R** as in Colonel
- **S** as in Island
- **T** as in Ballet
- **U** as in Ouija
- **V** as in Of
- **W** as in Wrong
- **X** as in Prix
- **Y** as in Key
- **Z** as in Rendezvous